The Life and Times
~ of the ~
HONEYBEE

Charles Micucci

TICKNOR & FIELDS BOOKS FOR YOUNG READERS   New York 1995

If little things with great we may compare,
Such are the bees, and such their busy care.

They work their waxen lodgings in their hives,
They labor honey to sustain their lives.

—Virgil (a Roman poet, 70-19 B.C.)
The Georgics

Ticknor & Fields
Books for Young Readers
A Houghton Mifflin company, 215 Park Avenue South,
New York, New York 10003

Manufactured in the United States of America
The text of this book is set in 22 point Plantin Light
The illustrations are watercolor, reproduced in full color

BVG   10   9   8   7   6   5   4   3   2   1

LIBRARY OF CONGRESS CATALOGING-IN-PUBLICATION DATA
Micucci, Charles.
The life and times of the honeybee / by Charles Micucci   p.   cm.

Summary: Depicts the life cycle and habits of the honeybee,
describing in detail the organization of the hive and the
making of honey.   ISBN 0-395-65968-X

1. Honeybee—Juvenile literature. 2. Bee culture—Juvenile literature.
3. Honey—Juvenile literature.   [Honeybee. 2. Bee culture. 3. Honey.]
I. Title.   QL568.A6M558 1994
595.79'9—dc20   93-8135   AC

Contents

A Honey of a Bee

For thousands of years the honeybee has been one
of our most valuable insects. It has supplied people
with honey for sweetening foods, and with beeswax
for candles and many other useful items. In addition,
the honeybee has helped farmers all over the world
to increase their fruit and vegetable harvests.

Rock paintings in Spain and Africa show that people collected honey over eight thousand years ago.

This rock painting shows a woman gathering honey. It was found near Valencia, Spain, and dates to around 6000 B.C.

Beeswax candles have a high melting point—146°F. Other candles, which melt at lower temperatures, may wilt as they burn.

Fruits such as apples would not grow in large numbers without honeybees to pollinate the blossoms.

Bees live in dark places. In the wild they often live in hollow trees. Through the ages people have housed honeybees in carved-out logs, clay pots, and straw skeps. Today, most beekeepers raise them in boxlike wooden hives.

Home Sweet Home

Honeybees live in a large group called a colony. Each colony occupies its own hive. Although there may be between ten thousand and sixty thousand bees in a colony, there are only three types of bees: workers, drones, and queens.

The workers are the smallest bees and they are female. Thousands of them perform chores in the hive. They make honey, clean the hive, feed larvae (baby bees), and build the wax comb, where all the bees live. Workers are the only honeybees that visit flowers.

Approximately one hundred drones live in each colony. They are male bees and mate with the queen.

The largest bee is the queen. Each colony has only one queen whose most important function is to lay eggs.

In the summer workers live for about six weeks. In the winter workers may live longer. Bees are less active then.

Drones live for about eight weeks in the summer. They usually leave the colony in the fall and die.

A healthy queen may live for up to four years and lay over one million eggs during that time.

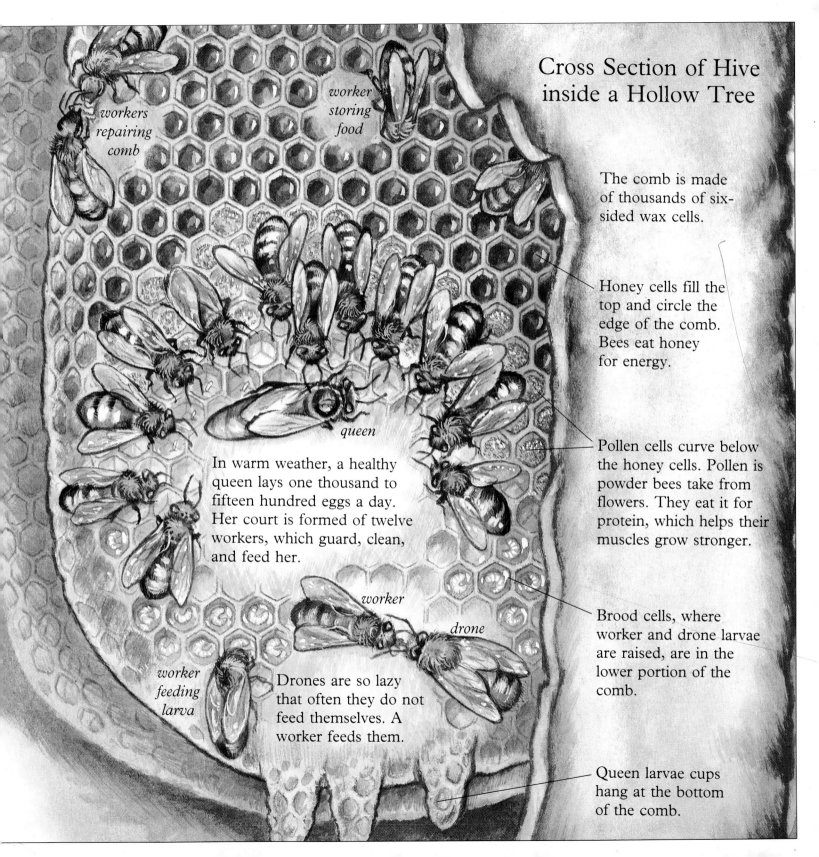

Cross Section of Hive inside a Hollow Tree

workers repairing comb

worker storing food

queen

In warm weather, a healthy queen lays one thousand to fifteen hundred eggs a day. Her court is formed of twelve workers, which guard, clean, and feed her.

worker

drone

worker feeding larva

Drones are so lazy that often they do not feed themselves. A worker feeds them.

The comb is made of thousands of six-sided wax cells.

Honey cells fill the top and circle the edge of the comb. Bees eat honey for energy.

Pollen cells curve below the honey cells. Pollen is powder bees take from flowers. They eat it for protein, which helps their muscles grow stronger.

Brood cells, where worker and drone larvae are raised, are in the lower portion of the comb.

Queen larvae cups hang at the bottom of the comb.

From Egg to Bee

Like many insects, a honeybee grows in four stages: egg, larva, pupa, and adult. The bee changes dramatically from one stage to the next.

Although all bees develop in the same four stages, the time it takes each type of bee to grow is different. Queens grow the fastest, in sixteen days. Workers mature in twenty-one days, and drones in twenty-four days.

A queen lays a soft, white, oval egg at the bottom of a cell in the comb.

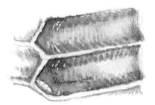

In three days, a wormlike form called a larva hatches from the egg.

Fed by worker bees, the larva grows much larger.

Then the larva spins a cocoon.

Inside the cocoon, a pupa develops from the larva. It starts to look more like an insect than like a worm. It grows eyes, legs, and wings.

Finally, an adult bee chews its way out of the cell.

Stages of growth:

	EGG	LARVA	PUPA	ADULT BEE
QUEEN	Days 1–3	Days 4–9	Days 10–15	Day 16
WORKER	Days 1–3	Days 4–9	Days 10–20	Day 21
DRONE	Days 1–3	Days 4–9	Days 10–23	Day 24

Young worker bees constantly care for and feed larvae. They feed royal jelly to queen larvae. They feed bee milk to worker and drone larvae for the first three days, and beebread after that.

Royal jelly is a milky, yellow syrup that young worker bees secrete from glands inside their heads. It is high in protein.

Bee milk is similar to royal jelly, but it is not as nutritious. It, too, comes from glands in the worker bee's head.

Beebread is a mixture of honey and pollen.

During its first day, a larva eats so much that its weight increases five and a half times. If the same thing happened to a boy who weighed 60 pounds on Monday, by Tuesday he would weigh 330 pounds.

The Worker Bee

When a worker crawls out of her cell, she is already fully grown. Even though she is one half-inch long and weighs only 1/250 ounce, she contributes more than any other type of bee to the daily survival of the colony.

A honeybee has two kinds of eyes: Two compound eyes with over three thousand lenses each allow the bee to see ultraviolet light, which is invisible to the human eye. With their ultraviolet vision, bees can see which flowers are full of nectar.

Three simple eyes act as light sensors. Bees can see the sun even when it is hidden by clouds.

THORAX

HEAD

regular vision   *ultraviolet vision*

Antennae detect scent like a nose does, and are used as feelers in the dark.

BEE JAWS

A bee uses her middle legs to brush pollen out of the thousands of branched hairs that cover her.

TONGUE

A bee uses her front legs like arms, to move flower parts and to dust off her antennae.

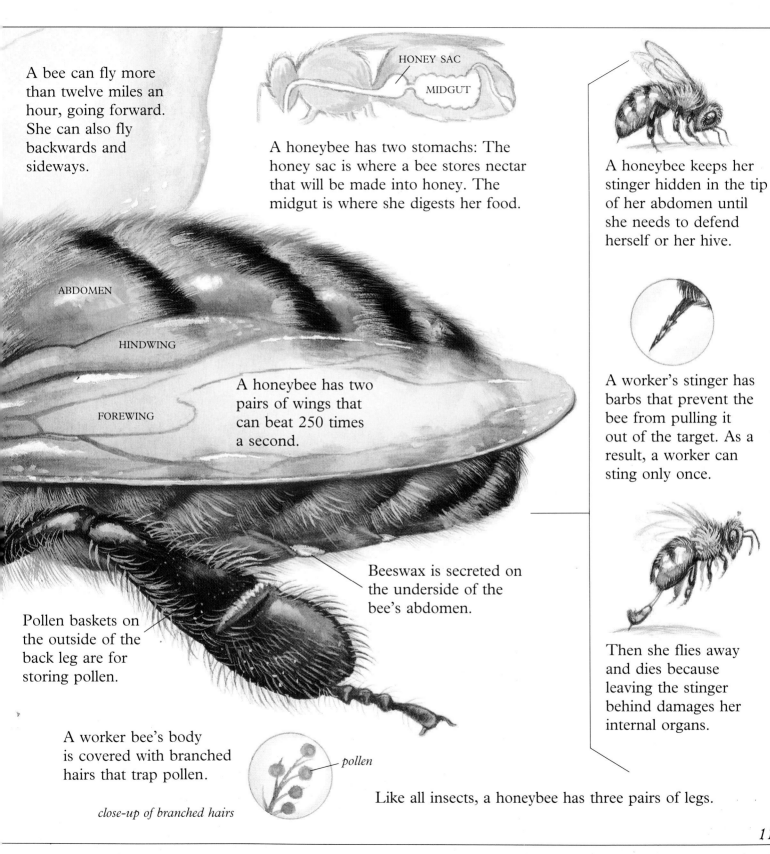

A bee can fly more than twelve miles an hour, going forward. She can also fly backwards and sideways.

HONEY SAC

MIDGUT

A honeybee has two stomachs: The honey sac is where a bee stores nectar that will be made into honey. The midgut is where she digests her food.

A honeybee keeps her stinger hidden in the tip of her abdomen until she needs to defend herself or her hive.

ABDOMEN

HINDWING

FOREWING

A honeybee has two pairs of wings that can beat 250 times a second.

A worker's stinger has barbs that prevent the bee from pulling it out of the target. As a result, a worker can sting only once.

Beeswax is secreted on the underside of the bee's abdomen.

Pollen baskets on the outside of the back leg are for storing pollen.

Then she flies away and dies because leaving the stinger behind damages her internal organs.

A worker bee's body is covered with branched hairs that trap pollen.

pollen

close-up of branched hairs

Like all insects, a honeybee has three pairs of legs.

11

The Busy Days of a House Bee

For the first three weeks of her adult life, a worker performs chores inside the hive. Beekeepers refer to these workers as house bees.

House bees clean the hive, feed larvae, build wax comb, store food, and defend the hive against enemies. No bee tells the house bees which chores need to be done. Instead, each bee is guided by an inner clock, and does certain chores as she reaches a certain age.

1–2 Days
When a worker bee is first born, she cleans her cell and the cells around it.

3–5 Days
When they are three days old, workers feed beebread to older drone and worker larvae.

beebread

6–11 Days

During this time, workers feed bee milk to young drone and worker larvae, and royal jelly to queen larvae.

bee milk

view showing white wax scales

12–17 Days

At this time, a bee's wax glands are the most active. Bees may hang from one another so that the wax flows more smoothly from their wax glands. Then, with her jaws, each bee shapes the wax into honeycomb.

a bee shaping wax with her jaws

Bees that are not making wax, store food in honeycombs. They deposit nectar (which will be made into honey) in honey cells, and pack pollen in pollen cells.

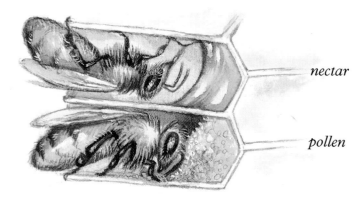

nectar

pollen

bees on guard as bear approaches

18–21 Days

During their last days in the hive, some workers guard the entrance. When alarmed, a guard bee emits a scent that warns the other bees of danger. A guard bee will give her life to protect the hive and its honey.

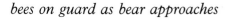

The Busy Days of a Field Bee

In the summer, during the last three weeks of her life, a worker bee leaves the hive and flies through fields, meadows, and gardens, visiting flowers. The worker has been a house bee. Now she becomes a field bee.

A field bee makes about ten journeys a day. Each flight lasts about an hour and is usually made within three miles of the bee's hive.

A field bee takes off on her first flight before dew dries on the flowers in the morning, and returns from her last trip at sunset. During her travels, a field bee gathers water, bee glue, nectar, and pollen, which the colony needs.

Buzz Note:
A field bee can visit ten flowers a minute, and may stop at over six hundred flowers before returning to the hive.

Water

A field bee collects water from small puddles. Water is used to thin honey that is too thick. Also, droplets are placed inside the hive in hot weather. The bees fan the water, which cools the hive as it evaporates.

Bee Glue

A field bee gathers sap from plant buds with her jaws, and stores it in her pollen baskets. Bees use the sap to seal cracks and to varnish the inside walls of the hive.

Nectar

Bees gather nectar, a sweet juice that oozes from flowers, and make it into honey. A field bee collects nectar by sitting still on a flower and sucking nectar with her tongue.

Pollen

A field bee gathers pollen from a flower by crawling over it. Pollen sticks to the bee's antennae and branched hairs. Then the bee hovers above the flower, and brushes the pollen into the pollen baskets on her hind legs.

nectar

bee dusting pollen off her antennae

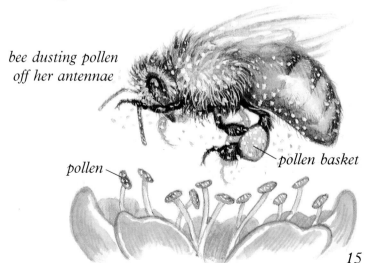

pollen

pollen basket

How Honeybees Make Honey

Making honey requires field bees and house bees. A field bee collects the nectar. When she returns to the hive, the house bees take over the process. They turn the nectar into honey.

With her ultraviolet vision, a field bee sees dark shapes that indicate which flowers are rich in nectar.

The field bee lands on the flower's petals and searches with her antennae for the sweet-smelling nectar.

honey sac

The field bee sucks up the nectar. The bee does not digest the nectar, but stores it in her honey sac.

While the field bee flies to the hive, her honey sac simplifies the sugar in nectar, so that it can change into honey.

When a field bee arrives at her hive, she transfers nectar to a house bee tongue-to-tongue.

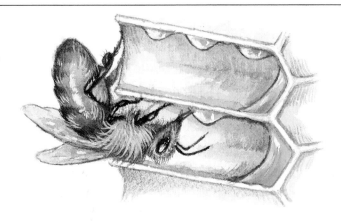

The house bee spreads a droplet of nectar on the roof of a honey cell, where the nectar begins to dry.

During the next couple of days, other house bees fan their wings over the honeycomb. Fanning evaporates the moisture in nectar, which is 80 percent water. Honey is only 19 percent water.

Finally, other house bees cap the honey cells with a thin layer of wax. Inside, the thickened nectar ages and becomes honey.

Buzz Note:
To make one pound of honey, a colony of bees collects nectar from over a million flowers.

Shall We Dance?

Field bees show other field bees where flowers are by dancing on the honeycomb in their hive. After the field bee has given the nectar to a house bee, she begins to walk rapidly in a circular pattern.

Other bees gather, and touch the dancing field bee with their antennae. By smelling the dancing bee, the other bees can tell what type of flowers she has visited. By feeling her movement, they can learn how far away the flowers are and, sometimes, their location. There are several bee dances, but the most common ones are the round dance and the tail-wagging dance.

Round Dance

The round dance says, "Flowers are close to the hive!" or less than one hundred yards away. The bee circles in one direction, then turns around and circles back in the other direction.

60 yards

The round dance does not show the exact location of the flowers so bees fly out in many directions looking for them, always staying within one hundred yards of the hive.

The Tail-Wagging Dance

The tail-wagging dance says, "Let me draw you a map, the flowers are a little further away!" or at least one hundred yards from the hive. The bee dances a half circle in one direction, turns, and runs straight while wagging her tail. Then she dances a half circle in the other direction.

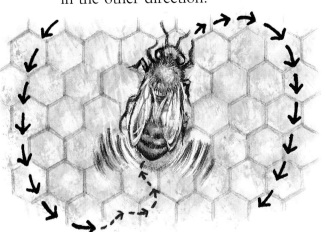

This dance shows both location and distance of the flowers, so the bees know exactly where to fly.

The direction of the tail-waggling run, in red, shows the location of the flowers in relation to the sun.

"Flowers are to the right of the sun."   "Flowers are to the left of the sun."

The number of waggle runs per fifteen seconds indicates the distance.

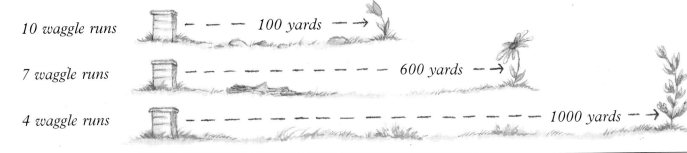

10 waggle runs   — — — 100 yards — →

7 waggle runs   — — — — — — 600 yards — →

4 waggle runs   — — — — — — — — 1000 yards — →

A Honey Flower Menu

There are many different colors and flavors of honey because bees collect nectar from many kinds of flowering plants.

sweet clover

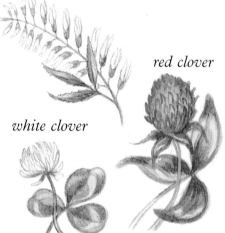

red clover

white clover

Clover honey is America's most popular honey. Clover grows in fields, along side roads, and in backyards.

Orange-blossom honey, valued for its fragrance is harvested in Florida and California.

Tupelo honey comes from trees that grow in swamps. Some tupelo beekeepers float their hives on rafts.

Buzz Note:
Most dark honeys have a stronger flavor than light honeys.

Buckwheat honey is one of the darkest honeys. People who enjoy its robust flavor may spoon it on hot cereal.

Apple-blossom honey is harvested by beekeepers after their bees have pollinated apple orchards.

 Sourwood honey is usually clear, but sometimes when harvested in eastern North Carolina it is blue-purple.

 Some **sunflowers** are over a foot in diameter and can be visited by many bees at a time.

 Eucalyptus honey comes primarily from Australia. Koala bears eat the leaves of the eucalyptus tree.

Sage nectar is made into honey by bees. Sage leaves are used as a spice in sausages and cheese.

 Avocado honey contains more minerals and vitamins than do most honeys. It is gathered in California.

Basswood honey is usually collected by beekeepers in June. It has a strong mint flavor.

beeline

 Goldenrod grows wild in fields and thickets. Its honey is used to sweeten graham crackers.

 Alfalfa is the world's oldest pasture crop. After bees visit alfalfa, it is cut and fed to horses and cows.

When a bee has collected enough nectar, it makes a "beeline" to the hive. That is the shortest distance from flower to hive.

A Honeybee Calendar

A bee hive is a busy place all year.

January
During the winter, workers stay inside the hive and huddle around the queen, vibrating against one another for warmth.

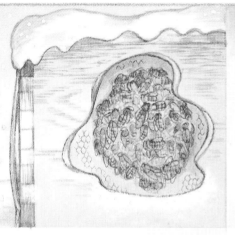

February
The queen bee starts laying eggs.

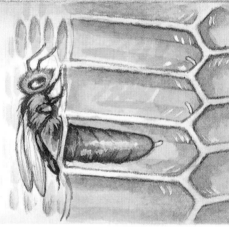

May
Late spring to early summer is swarming season. When a new queen is born, the old queen and about half the workers usually swarm out of the hive and look for a new home.

June
Worker bees collect nectar and pollen from white clover.

September
The drones are pushed out of the hive to die because they are no longer needed and they eat too much honey.

October
During their last flights of the season, bees gather nectar from goldenrod, asters, and other autumn flowers.

goldenrod

aster

As months change, so do many honeybee activities.

March

On the first day of the year when the temperature is above 54°F, worker bees fly out and begin to look for food

hazel catkins

April

Workers collect nectar and pollen from early-blooming flowers.

cherry blossoms

July

Beekeepers collect most honey during July, August, and September.

August

Workers prepare for winter by storing honey around the brood nest and filling cracks in the hive with bee glue to reduce drafts.

November

The queen stops laying eggs. As a result, her abdomen, which produces the eggs, may shrink.

abdomen   *before*

after

December

Once again, the workers crowd around the queen. During one winter a honeybee colony eats over fifty pounds of honey.

beehive wrapped in paper

The Honeybee's Best Friend

Throughout the year honeybees may face many hazards: freezing weather, scorching heat waves, and honey thieves, such as skunks and bears. Fortunately, honeybees have a friend—the beekeeper.

Beekeepers wrap paper around hives to keep them warm in winter, and place them in the shade near water during summer.

During spring, summer, and early fall, beekeepers may move their hives several times to place them near flowers that are full of nectar. Then, after the bees have filled the comb with honey, beekeepers harvest it. Some bee colonies produce over five hundred pounds of honey each year.

How beekeepers harvest honey:

When bees have capped most of the honeycomb cells, a beekeeper removes the comb from the hive.

The beekeeper uses an electric heat knife to melt the wax caps and open each honeycomb.

The honeycomb is then placed in an extractor that spins the honey and separates it from the comb.

Finally, the honey is strained through a metal screen and a cloth to filter out wax particles.

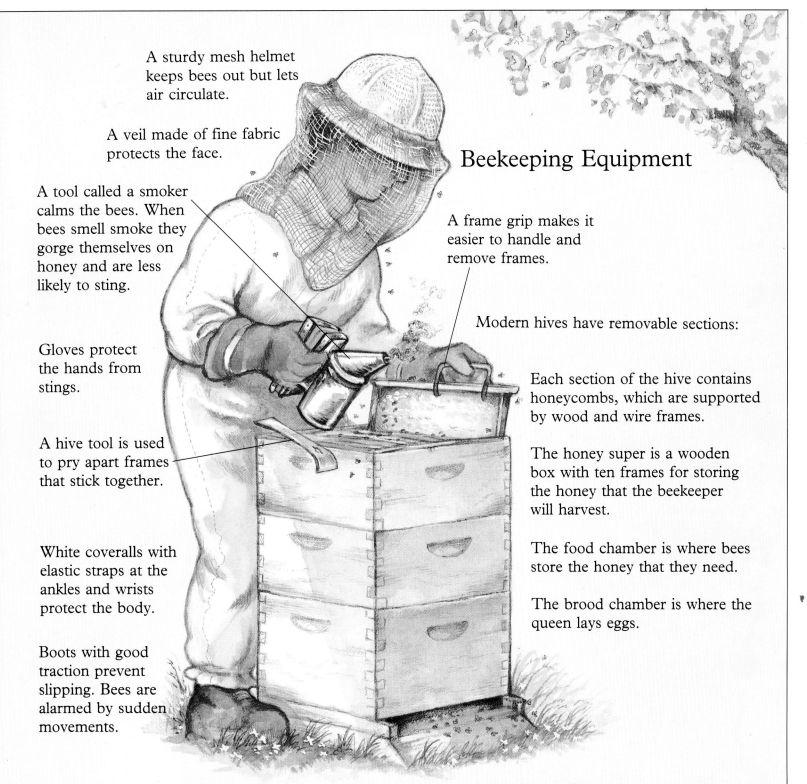

A sturdy mesh helmet keeps bees out but lets air circulate.

A veil made of fine fabric protects the face.

A tool called a smoker calms the bees. When bees smell smoke they gorge themselves on honey and are less likely to sting.

Gloves protect the hands from stings.

A hive tool is used to pry apart frames that stick together.

White coveralls with elastic straps at the ankles and wrists protect the body.

Boots with good traction prevent slipping. Bees are alarmed by sudden movements.

Beekeeping Equipment

A frame grip makes it easier to handle and remove frames.

Modern hives have removable sections:

Each section of the hive contains honeycombs, which are supported by wood and wire frames.

The honey super is a wooden box with ten frames for storing the honey that the beekeeper will harvest.

The food chamber is where bees store the honey that they need.

The brood chamber is where the queen lays eggs.

CAUTION: Honeybees can be dangerous. No one should disturb a bee or approach a beehive without a professional beekeeper's assistance.

blueberry

blackberry

 raspberry

strawberry

 pumpkin

 turnip

 almond

Golden Treasures of the Beehive

Beekeepers harvest a wide range of products from beehives. Honey sweetens many foods, including graham crackers, ice cream, and barbecue sauces. Beeswax is processed into candles, lipstick, and other useful items. Some beekeepers also harvest pollen, royal jelly, and bee glue.

However, the honeybee's greatest contribution isn't a product, it's a service—pollination. Honeybees pollinate more crops than any other insect. Without the honeybee, farmers would produce one third less fruits and vegetables than they do today.

 apple

 pear

Pollination

Peaches, like many other fruits and vegetables, cannot grow unless insects—usually honeybees—pollinate them. To pollinate a peach, a honeybee transfers the pollen from one peach blossom to another.

 squash

 cherry

 onion

 radish

 avocado

While a worker bee crawls around a peach blossom, the bee is dusted with pollen

The bee flies to another peach blossom, carrying pollen in her branched hair.

When the bee lands, pollen falls onto the new blossom's stigmas. Now a peach will grow.

 plum

 cranberry

 eggplant

 cucumber

 asparagus

 watermelon

Honey

Liquid honey can be spooned from glass jars or squeezed out of plastic bottles.

Comb honey is still in its original honeycomb, and is packed in a small wooden box.

Chunk honey is a piece of honeycomb with liquid honey poured over it.

Crystallized honey is thick and creamy, and is often sold in plastic tubs.

Beeswax

candles *lipstick* *artist's crayons* *shoe polish* *floor polish*

statues in wax museums *sealing wax* *buffing wax for skis and surfboards* *tree grafts*

Other products from the beehive

Bee pollen is used as a vegetarian protein supplement.

Royal jelly is sold in health food stores because it is believed to be nutritious.

Bee glue mixed with mineral spirits can be painted onto wood as a natural varnish.

27

Buzzing Around the World

Throughout the world, six million beekeepers care for over fifty million bee colonies. They use different techniques, but all together they harvest over one million tons of honey each year.

In England, some beehives have slanted roofs so rain drains off.

NORTH AMERICA

Canada is the world's fifth-largest honey-producer.

Flowers for perfume help make France Europe's leading honey-producer.

More than sixteen hundred migratory beekeepers truck their hives all over the U.S.

Over two hundred thousand beekeepers tending almost four million colonies make the U.S. the world's third-largest honey-producer.

Mexico is the world's fourth-largest honey-producer.

Most of the world's beeswax comes from Africa.

Beekeepers along the equator place their beehives on cedar stands to repel termites.

Killer bees escaped from a Brazilian laboratory in 1956

SOUTH AMERICA

The many pasture crops growing on the pampas make Argentina the leading honey-producer in South America

forest beekeeper
harvesting honey
from a tree

German bee house
containing many hives

EUROPE

The Russian republics are
the world's leading
honey-producers.

ASIA

For over two thousand years the
Chinese have raised two insects:
the honeybee and the silkworm.

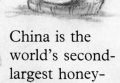

In Africa and Asia,
a bird known as
a honey guide leads
hunters to wild bee
colonies.

Mid-East
ceramic
pottery
hive

Nepal
honey
hunter

China is the
world's second-
largest honey-
producer.

AFRICA

Australian and New Zealand
beekeepers raise queen bees in
mini-hives. When the queens are
ready to lay eggs, they are sent
to beekeepers around the world.

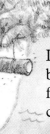

In the brushlands of Africa, many
beekeepers hang hollow log hives
from trees so that wild animals
cannot disturb the bees.

AUSTRALIA

100,000,000 B.C.
Bees and flowers evolved in the age of dinosaurs.

prehistoric bee trapped in amber

20,000,000 B.C.
Mammals replaced dinosaurs, and there was a new buzz in the air—honeybees.

8000 B.C.
After the Ice Age, people hunted bees with torches. The smoke calmed the bees so that people could take the honey. Modern beekeepers still use smoke to quiet bees.

Flying Through History

Honeybees are one of science's great mysteries, because they have remained unchanged for twenty million years, even though the world changed around them. People caused some of the biggest changes.

At first, people hunted bees and stole their honey. As the years passed, people learned to work with the bees. Eventually beekeepers and scientists discovered new and better honey-making techniques.

3000 B.C.
The ancient Egyptians are believed to have been the first beekeepers. They kept bees in mud and clay hives.

Buzz Note:
For thousands of years, honey and fruits were the only sweeteners in Europe. Sugar was not yet known there.

1500
In the Middle Ages, beekeepers wore straw masks and thick coats with hoods to protect themselves from stings. They kept bees in straw skeps, which were put in stone shelters called bee boles.

384–322 B.C.
The ancient Greeks, led by the philosopher Aristotle, studied new ways of raising bees.

50 B.C.
The Romans painted pictures with melted dyed beeswax.

skep

bee bole

1851–1852
Lorenzo Langstroth, a Philadelphia teacher and part-time beekeeper, invented the movable-frame beehive. Overnight, the beekeeping business boomed.

1873–1874
An Ohio beekeeper, A. I. Root, printed his bee knowledge using wind power. Today, his *ABC and XYZ of Bee Culture* is known as the beekeeper's encyclopedia.

1941–1945
During World War II, when sugar was rationed, Americans sweetened their food with honey.

1950s
Brother Adam, a monk from the Buckfast Abbey, England, began breeding bees that were resistant to diseases.

1700
Pioneers used boxes to trap honeybees. Then they released the bees, followed the beeline back to the hive, and took the honey.

1973
An Austrian zoologist, Karl von Frisch, won the Nobel Prize for discovering, among other facts, that bees dance to communicate.

1984
Honeybees constructed a honeycomb in zero gravity as part of an experiment on a space shuttle.

1638
Pilgrims brought the first honeybees to America. By the 1850s, honeybees had flown to California.

1992
Scientists discovered genes belonging to a bee that lived twenty-five million years ago.

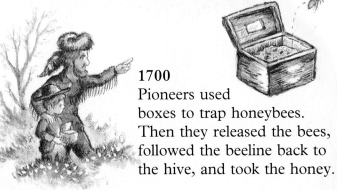

31

Today, honeybees fly on every continent except Antarctica. Wherever clover is scattered across a field or wild flowers brighten a hillside, honeybees collect nectar for honey, and pollen for their larvae. Buzzing sounds fill the air and add new chapters to the life and times of the honeybee.

Utah's State Flag

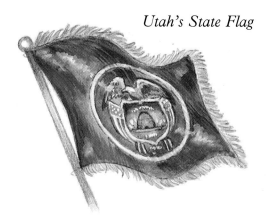

Utah is nicknamed the Beehive State. Ten other states (Arkansas, Mississippi, Missouri, Nebraska, New Jersey, North Carolina, Oklahoma, South Dakota, Vermont, and Wisconsin), list the honeybee as their official state insect.

The ancient Greeks minted coins with bees on them. Honeybees also appear on postage stamps. In fact, during the month of September, the Paris, Illinois, post office has a booth called Honey Bee Station.

The honeybee has long been a symbol of hard work. That's why someone who is working fast and hard is said to be "busy as a bee."